ARTISAN BREAD
COOKBOOK
FOR
BEGINNERS

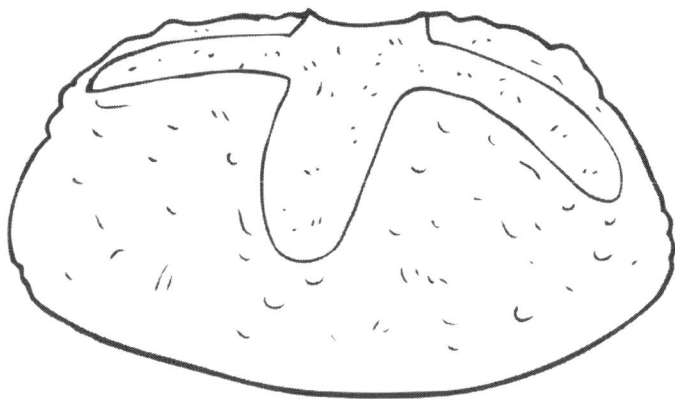

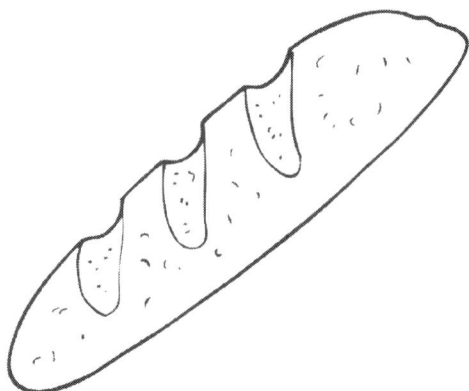

ARTISAN BREAD COOKBOOK FOR BEGINNERS

24 of the Best Beginner-Friendly Recipes with Cup Measurements, One Loaf Ingredients List, and Easy-to-Follow Instructions for Great Artisan Bread at Home

CAMILLE BOULANGER

CONTENTS

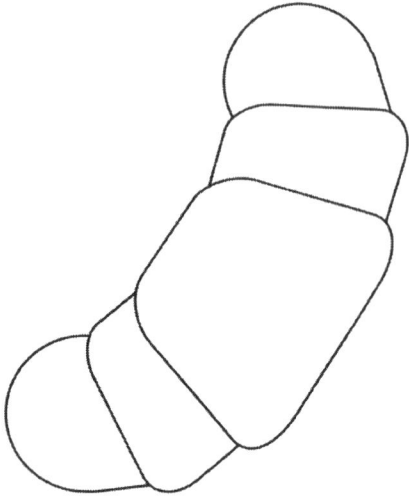

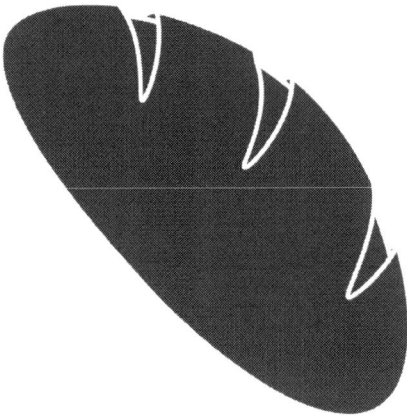

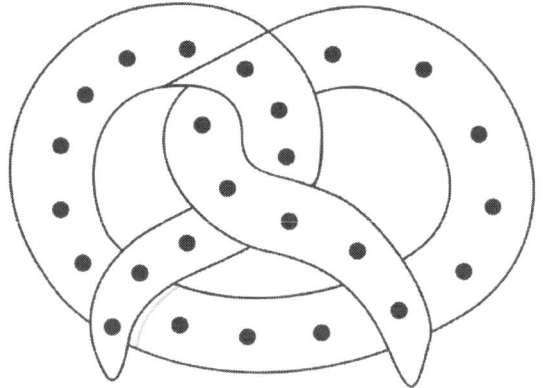

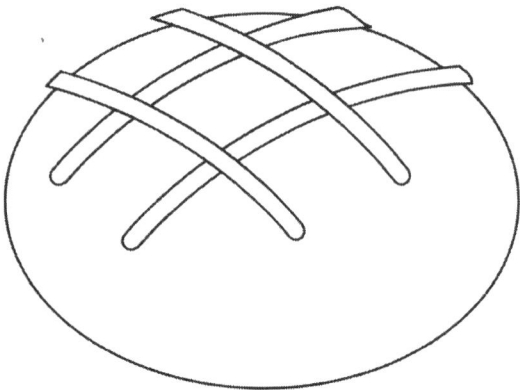

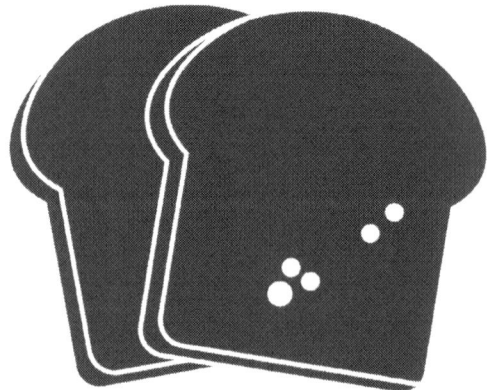

INTRODUCTION

Those wonderful aromas that greet you at the door of your local bakery and lingers long after you have eaten that crusty artisan bread you just had to buy. That is what prompts people to start baking their own bread.

So why have you not started baking yourself? The two most common answers for this question is artisan bread is too difficult to make unless you are an expert baker with many years under your belt. Yes, there are numerous artisan bread recipes in existence with many complicated steps and take a certain finesse. This book steers clear of those. To streamline the baking process, all measurements are standard measuring cups and spoons. Everything is easy and simple, without the intricate steps so you can create great looking and delicious artisan bread for everyone to enjoy.

The second drawback for the novice baker is the incredibly long rising times associated with artisan bread. Yes, there are plenty of recipes that have anywhere from 18 to 24 hours of rising time. The round-up of recipes included in this book have short rising times of about 4 hours.

These are the goals in place as the basis of this book. Fast and easy, with no hidden intricate steps that are off-putting to new bakers coupled with the information you need to start baking up a storm and inspire everyone you know to want to do the same.

CHAPTER 1

Basics to get started

When the baking bug has bitten, there are specific pieces of equipment, utensils, and everyday kitchen items that all bakers need. Some of these are already staples in your kitchen, while others are special for baking. Always start out with the must-haves, you can get the non-essentials as your experience in bread baking grows.

EQUIPMENT AND UTENSILS

Baking Pans

To enable you to start baking different types and styles of artisan bread, you need the following baking pans.

- Loaf pan
- Round cake pan
- Square
- Rectangular
- Baking sheet
- Muffin pan

Mixing Bowls

To start, you need at least two large mixing bowls, plus one medium-sized bowl.

Kitchen Scale

Kitchen scales are needed for precision measuring of ingredients, especially for very small amounts or when a recipe calls for ounces and when cups cannot be used.

Knives

Many recipes call for a lame to score bread before baking. This is a nice thing to have handy, but not essential. The two essential knives to have are a chef's knife and a serrated knife, and both these do the work of a lame very well.

Kitchen Towels

Most kitchens will have fabric kitchen towels. For this process, it's a good idea to always have a few on hand that are clean and ready to use when you start baking.

Measuring Cups and Spoons

Measuring cups are non-negotiable items when it comes to baking. You must have a good set for measuring liquids (these cups are designed to have extra space at the top to prevent spillage) and a set for measuring dry ingredients (straight top edge for easily leveling off ingredients with the back of a knife) accurately. A good set of measuring spoons is another essential, and make sure you buy a set that measures from the smallest available spoon measure up to a tablespoon.

Nonstick Spray

Keeping a container of nonstick spray on hand in the kitchen is always a great idea. Easy and convenient to use instead of butter and olive oil.

Ovens

The two methods of baking that are most popular in recipes for artisan bread are a stove oven and a Dutch oven. Investing in a good quality Dutch oven is not a needless expense as it is a workhorse and incredibly versatile not only for baking but for other food as well.

Paper Towels

Paper towels are one of those basic kitchen items we never really think about until you run out in the middle of baking and cooking. Always keep a roll handy when you start baking.

Parchment Paper

This is essential for baking many different types of bread. Simply place a sheet in your baking pan to prevent the bread from sticking, and it makes it easy to remove from the pan, especially large baked items. Parchment paper is an amazing helper for Dutch oven baking. Use this as a lining inside the pot, and make sure you use a generous sheet that folds up higher than the dough, creating a cradle for the bread. After baking, you use the edges of the paper as handles to easily and safely lift out the bread.

Pastry Brush

This is really a handy kitchen tool to have to coat the bread with egg wash, milk, butter, or whatever a specific recipe calls for. These brushes are not usually expensive, but in a pinch, when you do not have one, an unused toothbrush is useful as a stand-in.

Plastic Wrap

Plastic wrap is another of those items found in most kitchens with a list of uses that would be a mile long. Great for baking when you want the dough to rise with no mess, no fuss. Kitchen towels can be used for the same purpose. It is a good idea to keep a roll of plastic wrap in the kitchen as a fabric cloth does not work very well to prevent spillage.

Proofing Basket

A proofing basket is not essential when you start baking. You can use any bowl that can comfortably hold your dough or batter. This is one of those nice-to-have kitchen accessories.

Saucepan

You will need a medium-sized saucepan for all the artisan bread recipes that include ingredients that must be sautéed.

Scissors

Kitchen shears is another all-rounder kitchen utensil for cutting, snipping, and works well as a substitute for a lame in scoring bread by making a few snips across the top of the dough.

Spatulas and Scrapers

When it comes to spatulas and scrapers, you have a choice of rubber and silicone. It's a personal preference, but take note that silicone can withstand higher temperatures than rubber. Make sure that you have at least two before you start baking.

Stand Mixer

This is a good investment for any baker, especially when bread must be kneaded. You can knead by hand, but a stand mixer takes a lot of the heavy work off your hands. Invest in a mixer that has a dough hook attachment is the best option.

Thermometer

The best thermometer for baking is an instant-read thermometer. Some recipes call for this as it gives a more accurate temperature reading for those recipes that rely on the internal temperature of the item being baked.

Timer

Not all stoves have a built-in timer. This is an inexpensive item to add to your kitchen tools that helps to prevent baking disasters of overcooked and overly crisp bread and rolls.

Whisk

Wire whisks of various sizes are essential to any type of cooking and baking. Buy three different sizes and you are set to go.

Wire Cooling Rack

You need at least one wire cooling rack for baking. You cannot place your baked item on a solid surface to cool down as your bread will get soggy underneath.

Wooden Spoons

Long-handled wooden spoons have been around since before recorded history and with good reason. You need at the very minimum to have one long-handled wooden spoon for baking, but investing in a few good ones makes things easier as you don't have to keep cleaning the spoon before using it in another mixing bowl. These sturdy spoons are used for anything from stirring to working with dough.

STEPS IN BREAD MAKING

The following is your master list for successful baking. Every recipe won't include the steps below, some don't need kneading or folding or do not need all the different checks. The guideline is to assist you in baking artisan bread as an easy reference to make sure you have not forgotten a step, your checklist as you try out new recipes, and to make sure your favorite ones come out perfect each time.

Preparation

The first step is the most important step. Put all the ingredients in the recipe out on your counter or table and make sure everything you will need is there. The same goes for all equipment, appliances, and utensils needed for the specific recipe.

Measure or Weigh Ingredients

Use separate containers for measuring or weighing each ingredient and place the measured ingredients in the bowls. Being methodical also acts like a check because you will immediately see if you have missed an ingredient.

Combine, Mix, and Knead

The next step is to place the ingredients into the mixing bowl in the order specified in the recipe. Mix the yeast ingredients and let it rest if the instructions say to. Then add the other ingredients and combine the ingredients with the yeast mixture. Next, come mixing with a wooden spoon or use a stand mixer until everything is thoroughly mixed. For no-knead bread recipes, this step ends here. For the bread that must be kneaded, turn the mixture out onto a floured work surface and knead according to the recipe.

First Rising

This is often referred to as a resting period. The first rising is to allow the dough to rise and is needed to aerate the bread dough until it has doubled in size. Skipping this step will result in flat, clay-like bread that is very unappetizing. Place the dough in a floured or greased bowl, cover and set aside in a warm place in the kitchen and leave it undisturbed to rise.

Stretch, Fold, Punch Down, and Shape

After the first rising period, the dough must be reworked. The recipe and type of bread you are making will determine how this step progresses. For kneaded bread, this is where you punch down the dough. Certain recipes require stretching the dough to improve elasticity and extra kneading. The dough is shaped, and you will place it on a baking sheet, or put it back into the greased bowl, or into a greased loaf pan. If you have a proofing basket, place the dough into the basket for the second rising. With Dutch oven baking, most recipes tell you to put the dough into the Dutch oven for the second rising phase.

Second Rising

The second rising or proofing period again allows the dough to double or nearly double in size. This phase is needed to ensure the bread has a light and airy texture instead of being very dense.

First Check

If you are unsure whether the dough has risen sufficiently and is properly aerated, pinch off a small piece of the dough and place it into a glass filled with water. Dough that is fully aerated and has formed sufficient air bubbled inside the dough will rise to the surface and is ready for the next step in baking. Should the dough sink down, you should extend the rising time. Start with 30 minutes of extra rising time and check again. This part can be repeated until the dough is ready.

Preheat

Preheating of the oven is done during the second rising at roughly 30 minutes before the end of the rising period. This allows enough time for the oven to heat up to the exact degrees required for the recipe.

Second Check

You perform a second check before the dough goes into the oven for baking. Press into the dough with a finger, and if the texture feels airy and reminds you of pressing a marshmallow between your fingers, then the bread is ready for the oven. There is nothing wrong with your dough or with your baking experience if the dough needs extra rising time. Many factors influence how fast and good dough rises on any particular day.

Bake

For oven baking, the baking pan will go into the oven onto the oven rack, and if using a Dutch oven, the Dutch oven containing the bread dough will be placed into the oven. Baking time is according to specific recipes. For oven-baked bread, the easiest check is to knock on the bottom of the bread with your knuckles, and if it sounds hollow, the bread is done. If you don't hear that sound, place the bread back into the oven and bake for 5-10 minutes longer.

Third Check (For Dutch Oven Baking)

This check is specifically for bread baked in Dutch ovens. Halfway through the baking time you must remove the lid from the Dutch oven and continue baking uncovered. This allows a crust to form.

Cool Down

This is the final step of baking. Remove the bread from the oven and place it on a wire cooling rack. Please do not let it cool down on a solid surface as this will spoil the bread and turn that lovely crust at the bottom of the loaf soggy and unappetizing. Some recipes will specify to allow the bread to cool down completely. This is necessary for some bread recipes to allow the bread to settle so that it can be sliced without the bread crumbling.

CHAPTER 2

COMMON MISTAKES

Mistakes happen all the time in baking and sometimes result in the best creations. Nobody is born with the knowledge and skills to be a great baker. The most important thing is to learn from the mistakes others have made. This makes your own journey into creating great homemade bread so much easier, less stressful, and a whole lot of fun.

TAKE NOTES

Taking notes may seem old fashioned and a waste of time when you have the recipe in front of you. Professional bakers do this all the time, so learn from them. Jotting notes down help you improve for future use of a specific recipe such as is the texture too crumbly, or too dense, did you have to allow extra rising time, or you might need to add extra salt.

SWITCHING FLOUR

Recipes are created with specific flour in mind. Usually, recipes will indicate what flour types can be substituted successfully. Flour can become tricky as different types have different levels of protein and also need different amounts of liquid. Substituting flour that is not compatible with the recipe can result in flat and very dense bread. It is far safer to look for a method for the specific flour you wish to use.

DIFFERENT FORMS OF YEAST

The two types of yeast most often used in making artisan breads are instant yeast and active dry yeast, and the preparation differs from each other.

- Instant yeast tells you exactly what it is. There is no need for mixing it with water and allowing it to proof. You add the dry granules directly to the flour mixture.

- Active dry yeast must be mixed with water, according to the instructions in the recipe and set aside to develop before being added to the other dry ingredients.

DENSE BREAD

The two main reasons bread turns out too dense comes down to a mixing mistake and the expiry dates of commercial yeast.

It is important to understand that when salt and yeast come into direct contact with each other, there is a negative reaction. That is why many recipes specifically tell you to add the yeast granules to one side of the mixing bowl and the salt on the opposite side of the bowl. This allows the flour in the bowl to act as a barrier when you mix the dough. Make it a rule right from the start of your baking to never put salt directly onto yeast, and you will eliminate this problem immediately.

The other reason for bread being too dense is not checking the expiry date on your packets of yeasts. Never use yeast past its expiry date as this is a recipe for disaster. Instead, buy fresh yeast as and when you need it instead of stockpiling.

MEASURE AND WEIGHT

To bake perfect bread, you must correctly measure or weigh each ingredient according to the recipe. Making bread takes a lot of effort and time that will be wasted if you add even a few ounces or an extra scoop of flour as the texture of the bread can change radically.

MAKING DOUGH TOO DRY

Dough texture differs from one recipe to another, and often the perfect dough for that recipe is rather sticky. This is something many bakers are not comfortable with, and they keep adding flour until the dough is, to their way of thinking, easier to handle. Follow the recipe instructions step. If you think the mixture is too wet or sticky the first time you make a recipe, make notes, but keep to the recipe and see how the bread comes out.

You can always adjust the flour ratio for the next time if you are not happy with the final result of the bread.

TOO IMPATIENT TO WAIT

Impatience is the downfall of many aspiring bakers. You want to bake and do it in the fastest time possible. Again, recipes are created with specific proofing time, and taking shortcuts is simply not worth it. Dough that has not risen properly will not make delicious, puffy bread. If a recipe asks for too long a rising period to suit your needs, instead use a recipe with a shorter rising time.

BOTTOM CRUSTS BURNED

When the bottom crust of the bread is burned, and the rest of the bread isn't cooked thoroughly, it means the oven rack was too near the stove element. The best position to bake any bread is on the center rack of the oven.

BREAD BROWNS TOO FAST

When the bread browns faster than it should according to the specified baking time, do not be tempted to take the bread out of the oven as it needs the full baking time to allow the bread to bake through properly. To prevent it from burning, make a tent of foil and place it over the bread, and continue to bake for the full baking time.

SCORING

Scoring the bread is not simply a decoration, it is essential for most artisan loaves. The scoring creates vents for the internal gases to escape, and forgetting to score the bread could result in the crusts on the sides of the breast cracking open. Unscored bread does not rise fully and spoils the look of the bread.

TEMPERATURES

The topic of temperatures is debated endlessly amongst professional bakers. The temperatures of the yeast, of dough, water, the ambient temperature in the kitchen, and the oven temperatures are questioned and calculated. When a beginner is faced with these different calculations offered by professionals, it can turn them off baking for good.

The best way to start out making bread is to follow exactly the temperatures given in a recipe.

- Never use boiling water; the general rule of thumb is to use water 100-130 degrees F.

- Always use ingredients at room temperature, as stated in recipes. Using ingredients straight from the refrigerator instead of allowing it to come to room temperature can influence the texture and taste of the final product.

- Follow baking temperatures strictly. The recipe calculates temperature and baking times, specifically for each recipe or optimal results.

- Baking at high altitudes does influence bread making. The dough tends to rise very fast. There is no exact formula for high altitude baking as it differs from place to place. Two things to try are to reduce the yeast quantity by ¼ and to lower the oven temperature. Taking notes is hugely helpful to get the exact changes needed to perfect high-altitude cooking.

CHAPTER 3

DUTCH OVEN BAKING

Artisan bread loves a Dutch oven. It is easy and no fuss and gives you lovely round loaves suitable for any meal or snack. It is always a good idea to use parchment paper in the Dutch oven to help you lift out the baked bread without burning yourself or damaging the bread. Use a large enough sheet of parchment paper so that you lift the bread out, it is cradled in the parchment paper.

EASY HOMEMADE BREAD

Prep Time: 4 hours and 10 minutes

Baking Time: 50 minutes

Total Time: 5 hours

Makes: 1 loaf

Equipment: Dutch oven, parchment paper

Ingredients:

- 1 ½ cups all-purpose flour
- ½ cups whole wheat flour (ratios can differ so long as it is 3 cups altogether)
- 1 ¼ tsp salt, kosher or sea salt
- ⅜ tsp active dry yeast (or use ¼ tsp instant yeast)
- 1 ¾ cups lukewarm water (do not use hot water)

Instructions:

1. Place yeast, salt, and flour in a large mixing bowl and mix together.

2. Pour warm water into the mixing bowl and stir. The dough must be sticky, if it is not, then add small amounts of water until it has a sticky consistency.

3. Cover the mixing bowl with a clean kitchen towel or plastic wrap and set aside in a warm place in the kitchen for the dough to rest for about 3 hours. The dough should show holes left where bubbles had formed and popped, or have bubbles on the surface.

4. Sprinkle a working surface with flour and turn the dough ball out onto that.

Fold the dough over twice onto itself before forming a loaf shape. Place the loaf on a piece of parchment paper, making sure the seam is at the bottom of the dough. Fold the parchment paper over until you have a neat, loaf shape.

5. Place dough loaf on a counter and cover with a clean kitchen towel. Leave it to rise for 1 ½ - 2 hours.

6. About 30 minutes before the loaf will be ready to bake, place the Dutch oven into your stove oven and set the temperature to 450 degrees F.

7. Your loaf is ready when you nudge the dough with your finger, and the dough does not immediately spring back. Score the loaf with a lame or a sharp kitchen knife across the top, a few cuts only.

8. Carefully pick up the loaf by the corners of the parchment paper and place it into the Dutch oven. Do not remove the paper. Place the covered Dutch oven into the stove and bake bread for 30 minutes. Remove the lid and place back into the oven and bake for a further 15-20 minutes.

9. Turn the bread out onto a wire cooling rack.

CRUSTY FRENCH BREAD

Prep Time: 1 hour and 30 minutes

Baking Time: 45 minutes

Total Time: 2 hours and 15 minutes

Servings: 1 loaf

Equipment: Dutch oven, electric mixer fitted with a dough hook (optional, dough can also be mixed by hand)

Ingredients:

- 2 ½ cups of all-purpose flour (plus extra to dust the work surface)
- 1 ¼ cups warm water (max 100 degrees F)
- 2 ¼ tsp active dry yeast
- 1 ½ tsp salt (your own choice of type)
- 1 tsp sugar

Instructions:

1. Place, sugar, yeast, and warm water into the bowl of the mixer or into a large mixing bowl and allow the yeast mixture to proof. After 5 minutes check and if the yeast is foamy, it is ready to be used.

2. Add flour and salt to the yeast mixture slowly and mix on low speed. When the dough starts pulling away from the sides of the mixing bowl, it is ready. If mixing by hand, only mix until the ingredients have combined and formed a smooth ball of dough.

3. Lightly flour the top and sides of the dough. Do not mix it in, as this flour is to prevent the dough from sticking in the bowl. Turn the dough ball over and sprinkle the sides that have not been floured.

4. Cover the bowl with a kitchen towel and set aside on a counter for the dough to rise until the dough has doubled in size, approximately 1 hour.

5. When the dough is ready, lightly flour a large cutting board and place the dough on the cutting board by turning the mixing bowl upside down. Handle the dough gently and never punch the dough down, or you will lose the airy texture of the bread. If the dough sticks in the bowl, wet your hands to make sure you get all the dough out of the bowl.

6. Sprinkle extra flour over the top of the dough ball and shape into a round bread loaf. Place the loaf into a floured proofing basket or any smallish mixing bowl that will hold the loaf and make sure the dough is seam-side down. Cover with a kitchen towel or plastic wrap and set aside for about 30 minutes for the final rising.

7. While the bread is doing the final rising, place your Dutch oven, with the lid on into your oven and set the temperature to 460 degrees F.

8. When the oven is hot, and the bread is ready to be baked, remove the Dutch oven carefully from the oven (use oven gloves) and remove the lid.

9. Tip the dough carefully out of the proofing basket onto the floured cutting board and place the bread into the Dutch oven, taking care that the seam is now on top. You could use parchment paper to make it easier, and form a cradle for the dough to place it inside the Dutch oven.

If you use parchment paper, leave it in the Dutch oven, you will pull this off once the bread is baked.

10. Place the lid on the Dutch oven and place it in the stove oven to bake for 30 minutes.

11. After 30 minutes, remove the lid from the Dutch oven. At this stage, the bread should be slightly brown and have a good crust. Put the uncovered Dutch oven back into your oven and bake for 10-20 until the bread is a deeper shade of brown, and the crust is very crisp.

12. When the bread is fully baked, remove the Dutch oven from the oven and use a spatula with a long handle to help you take the bread out. Place the bread on a wire rack to cool.

CINNAMON RAISIN BREAD

Prep Time: 1 hour

Baking Time: 40 minutes

Total Time: 1 hour and 40 minutes

Servings: 1 loaf

Equipment: Dutch oven, electric mixer, parchment paper

Ingredients:

- 1 ½ cups warm water
- 3 cups all-purpose flour (can be substituted with whole wheat flour or gluten-free flour)
- 3 tbsp brown sugar
- 2.3 cup raisins
- 1 ½ tsp instant yeast
- 2 tsp cinnamon
- ½ tsp salt

Instructions:

1. Place the warm water and yeast into the bowl of an electric mixer and stir. Set aside for 5 minutes to give the yeast time to activate.

2. Add the flour, sugar, cinnamon, salt, and raisins to the mixing bowl and mix on slow speed with the dough attachment. Once the dough comes together, check to see if it is too wet or too dry. Add either water or flour one 1 tbsp at a time until the dough is an even consistency.

3. Lightly flour a workspace and toss the dough until the dough ball is covered in flour, and then put the dough into a greased mixing bowl. Cover the bowl with a kitchen towel or plastic wrap and set aside in a warm part of the kitchen to rise until its size has doubled about 1 hour.

4. Preheat the oven while the dough is rising to 450 degrees F.

5. Cut a sheet of parchment paper big enough to hold the dough with enough paper to fold the paper up against the sides of the Dutch oven.

6. Place the dough in the middle of the parchment paper and give the top of the dough a dusting of flour. Handle the dough minimally and use the parchment paper to lift the dough and place it in the Dutch oven and put the lid on.

7. Bake the bread covered for 30 minutes, then remove the lid and continue baking uncovered for 10 more minutes, or until the crust is light brown.

8. Remove the bread from the Dutch oven by using the parchment paper to prevent burning yourself and place it on a wire cooling rack for 10 minutes before serving.

Notes:
1. This bread freezes very well, either as a loaf or sliced.
2. The loaf will stay fresh for 3-5 days stored in an airtight container.

OATMEAL BREAD

Prep Time: 3 hours

Baking Time: 1 hour and 10 minutes

Total Time: 4 hours and 10 minutes

Servings: 1

Equipment: Dutch oven, dough scraper

Ingredients:

- 1 cup wholegrain oats
- 3 cups flour, plus extra for dusting
- 1 ¾ cups water
- ¼ tsp dry active yeast
- 1 ½ tsp sea salt or kosher salt (or personal preference)

Instructions:

1. Place oatmeal, 3 cups of flour, salt, and yeast into a mixing bowl. Add the water to the dry mixture and stir until well mixed. Cover the mixing bowl with plastic wrap and set aside in a part of the kitchen that is warm. Leave to rise for 3 hours.

2. Place a large sheet of parchment paper on a work surface, as well as an unused mixing bowl.

3. The dough is ready when the surface is flat, and small bubbles show on top of the dough.

4. Prepare a well-floured work surface and using a dough scraper, transfer the dough to the floured area. Please note that this is a very sticky and wet dough, so you will need a scraper.

5. Use the scraper to fold the dough over 10-12 times and transfer the dough to the parchment paper. Fold the sides of the parchment paper up and place the paper-wrapped dough into the clean mixing bowl. Cover the bowl with a kitchen towel or plastic wrap and set aside for the dough to rise for another 30-35 minutes.

6. Place a Dutch oven, with the lid on into the oven and heat the oven to 450 degrees F. (This is extremely hot, please do not handle the hot dutch oven without proper oven mitts).

7. Remove the Dutch oven from the stove oven. Pick up the dough ball by the edges of the parchment paper and place the dough still wrapped in the paper, inside the Dutch oven and add the lid.

8. Bake for 30 minutes, then remove the Dutch oven from the stove oven, lift out bread and remove the parchment paper from the bread.

9. Place bread back into the Dutch oven and bake uncovered for a further 10 minutes. If you like the crust to be extra crisp, extend the baking time. Test the bread to see if it is done by tapping the bread on the bottom. If you hear a hollow sound, it means the bread is done.

10. Place bread on a wire cooling rack before serving.

11. This bread can be stored in an airtight container for up to 3 days.

CHEDDAR AND JALAPEÑO BREAD

Prep Time: 1 hour and 30 minutes

Baking Time: 50 minutes

Total Time: 2 hours and 20 minutes

Servings: 1 loaf

Equipment: Dutch oven, rubber or silicone spatula

Ingredients:

- 2 cups warm water
- 3 ½ cups (extra flour to use to dust the dough)
- 2 ½ cups sharp cheddar cheese, shredded
- 1 jalapeño sliced into thin rings and separated
- 2 jalapeños, chopped, remove seeds
- 2 ¼ tsp instant yeast
- 1 tbsp sea salt or kosher salt
- 1 tbsp olive oil

Instructions:

1. Place the bread flour, the chopped jalapeños, and 2 cups of cheddar cheese into a large mixing bowl and stir lightly.

2. Place the yeast and the warm water into a separate mixing bowl and stir. Then add the flour mixture to the bowl of yeast and water. Use a spatula to stir the mixture until it forms a dough that holds together.

3. Fold the dough with the spatula, moving the dough from the edges of the mixing bowl, working it towards the center. Each time you fold the dough towards the center, rotate the bowl. Repeat this folding and rotation action 8 times.

4. Cover the bowl with plastic wrap or a kitchen towel and set aside in a warm place in the kitchen to rise until about doubled in size, about 60 minutes.

5. Then repeat the folding of the dough 8 times, recover the bowl, and set aside to rise for another 30 minutes.

6. Place the Dutch oven, lid on in the stove oven, and preheat the oven for 30 minutes to 450 degrees F.

7. Prepare a clean workspace and flour it lightly. Set a small flat dish at the side with flour to dip your hands into before working with the dough.

8. Cut a large square of parchment paper, big enough for the dough to rest in the center with enough parchment paper to lift up and cover the dough.

9. Carefully remove the dough from the mixing bowl and place it on the floured workspace. Fold the dough over 8 times by taking the edges up and pulling it towards the center. Then place the dough in the center of the parchment paper.

10. Use olive oil to brush the top of the dough. This is important as the oil helps the cheese to stick to the dough. Sprinkle ½ cup of cheddar cheese over the top of the dough and score the bread twice with a lame or a sharp kitchen knife. The scoring is important as it acts as vents for escaping steam from within the bread. Lastly, place the jalapeño slices over the cheese.

11. Remove the hot Dutch oven from the oven and lift up the dough by the edges of the parchment paper and place it into the pot and place the lid on the Dutch oven. Bake the bread covered for 30 minutes. Remove the lid and bake uncovered for a further 20 minutes. Bread is done when the crust is golden brown.

12. Remove the bread from the pot and place it onto a cooling rack. Carefully remove the parchment paper and allow the bread to cool down for 1 hour; this settles the bread and makes it easier to slice.

CHAPTER 4

NO-KNEAD ARTISAN LOAVES

This type of artisan bread is very popular worldwide as it takes away the burden of kneading, stretching, and punching down the dough.

CRUSTY WHITE BREAD MASTER RECIPE

You can make a large amount of dough as this dough stays fresh in the fridge for up to 14 days. Should you wish to make the dough for later use, make sure that you place the dough in separate containers, each container holding the dough for 1 loaf. This recipe is suitable for variations without changing the basic ingredient amounts. Add herbs and spices as per personal preference or add toasted seeds as a topping before baking.

Prep Time: 2 hours
Baking Time: 30-35 minutes
Total Time: 2 hours and 40 minutes
Servings: 1 loaf
Equipment: Dutch oven, proofing basket

Ingredients:
- ¾ cup of warm water
- 1 ⅔ cups all-purpose flour, unbleached (measure the flour by scooping it up and leveling the top of the cup measure with a blunt knife)
- 1 ¼ tsp sea salt or kosher salt
- ¾ tsp active dry yeast
- Cornmeal to dust the loaf (optional as the all-purpose flour can be used)

Instructions:

1. Mix the salt, yeast, and warm water in a large mixing bowl. It is okay if all the yeast does not dissolve, it will become incorporated in the dough.

2. Add all the flour to the yeast mixture all at once and use a wooden spoon to stir the mixture. This is a very wet and shapeless dough, so if it becomes difficult to stir, then wet your hands and press the dough together. Do not knead the dough, pressing the dough together is only to make sure there are no blobs of dry flour left. This dough should be floppy and wet.

3. Cover the mixing bowl with a kitchen towel and set aside to let the dough rise for 2 hours.

4. After 2 hours of rising, the dough is ready to be used. The dough will be sticky at this stage, so handle the dough with wet hands.

5. Place the Dutch oven with lid into the oven and heat to 450 degrees F.

6. Place the dough ball in the middle of a large sheet of parchment paper and use kitchen shears to snip the top of the dough a few times, for air vents.

7. Remove the Dutch oven from the oven. Lift up the dough by holding onto the edges of the parchment paper and put it into the Dutch oven and put the lid on the pot.

8. Bake the bread for 20 minutes and then remove the lid from the Dutch oven and continue baking uncovered until the crust is a firm and deep brown.

9. When the crust is a deep brown, remove the Dutch oven from the oven and check to see if the bread is done. If you hear a hollow sound when you tap the bottom of the loaf, the bread is done.

10. Place the bread on a wire cooling rack and allow it to cool down before serving.

Notes:

1. If you have made the dough in bulk, or simply made the dough for 1 loaf to be used later, place the container in the fridge, but do not seal the container. Just cover the bowl with plastic wrap, but do not seal it around the bowl. The dough becomes easier to handle after it has been refrigerated as it becomes less sticky with extra resting time.

2. It is important to note that if the dough is refrigerated, it will look like it has deflated and shrunk a bit, that is normal. Please do not punch down the refrigerated dough, as this will expel the gas from inside the dough and the bread will come out dense.

3. When you make the dough in bulk, it is advisable to separate balls of dough into 1 loaf quantities to store in the fridge as it is easier to use.

4. When using refrigerated dough, place the dough on a workspace that has been dusted with flour. Also, dust your hands with flour as it makes handling the dough easier. Stretch the dough very gently and pull the edges towards the center and tuck edges underneath the dough ball. Place the dough into a proofing basket that has been dusted with flour and let the dough rest for about 40 minutes before baking the bread.

NO YEAST MULTI-SEED BREAD

Prep Time: 10 minutes

Baking Time: 45 minutes

Total Time: 55 minutes

Servings: 1 loaf

Equipment: 5 x 9-inch loaf pan, nonstick baking spray

Bread Ingredients:
- 1 ¼ cup all-purpose flour
- ½ cup sunflower seeds, toasted
- ¾ cup whole-wheat flour
- 2 tbsp sesame seeds
- 2 tbsp black sesame seeds
- ½ cup pumpkin seeds, toasted
- ½ tsp salt
- ½ tsp baking soda
- 1 tsp baking powder
- 1 egg, bring it to room temperature before using
- ¼ cup honey
- 1 ¼ cup buttermilk, bring to room temperature before using
- ¼ cup sunflower oil

Topping Ingredients:

- 1 tbsp sunflower seeds, toasted
- ½ tbsp black sesame seeds
- 1 tbsp pumpkin seeds, toasted
- ½ tbsp sesame seeds

Instructions:

1. Preheat the oven to 350 degrees F.

2. Put all the seeds for the bread, baking powder, both types of flour, salt, and baking soda into a large mixing bowl and stir well with a wooden spoon.

3. Use a second mixing bowl and put the egg, honey, buttermilk, and sunflower oil in it. Use a wire whisk to combine the wet ingredients.

4. Transfer the wet mixture into the mixing bowl holding the dry ingredients. Gently mix the bread batter with a wooden spoon until just combined. Do not beat or whisk the bread batter as this will change the texture of the bread from soft, moist bread to a hard, chewy bread.

5. Use nonstick baking spray or butter to grease a 5x9-inch loaf pan.

6. Pour the bread batter into the prepared loaf pan and even out the top of the bread with a spoon and finish off by sprinkling the topping mixture over the top.

7. Place the loaf pan in the center of the oven and bake for 45 minutes. Check that the bread is fully cooked and golden brown before removing from the oven.

8. Place the bread on a wire cooling rack and allow it to cool down completely before slicing as the bread could tear or crumble when sliced while still hot.

9. This bread is suitable for sandwiches, toast, or with butter.

NUTTY FRUIT BREAD

Prep Time: 4 hours and 10 minutes

Baking Time: 30 minutes

Total Time: 4 hours and 50 minutes

Servings: 1 loaf

Equipment: Dutch oven, dough scraper, parchment paper

Ingredients:

- 1 ½ cups bread flour (all-purpose flour can be used as well)
- 2 tbsp flour for working and shaping the dough
- 1 ½ cups warm water (max 130 degrees F)
- 1 ½ cups whole wheat flour
- 3 tbsp sugar (if you prefer a sweeter load, add 4 tbsp of sugar instead of 3 tbsp)
- ¼ tsp of active dry yeast or instant yeast
- ½ to ⅔ cup raisins
- 1 tsp salt
- ½ cup walnuts, chopped

Instructions:

1. Put yeast, flour, raisins, sugar, walnuts, and salt into a large mixing bowl and stir to mix. Add water gradually to the mixture until the dough is mixed thoroughly. If you use active dry yeast, place the yeast, flour, and water into a small mixing bowl and set aside for 10 minutes for the yeast to bloom. Then add the yeast mixture to the bowl holding the raisins, walnuts, sugar, and

salt.

2. Cover the bowl with plastic wrap or a kitchen towel and set aside for 3 hours to rise at room temperature.

3. The dough is ready when the surface of the dough shows bubbles and has risen. Place the dough on a work surface that has been floured. Dust the dough with flour and fold over with a scraper. Repeat this 10-12 times, and shape dough with your hands into a ball.

4. Line a bowl with parchment paper and place the dough inside the bowl. Cover the bowl with a kitchen towel or plastic wrap and set aside for 35 minutes.

5. Preheat the oven to 450 degrees F and place a Dutch oven with a lid inside the oven to heat up.

6. When the dough is ready, remove the Dutch oven from the stove and place the dough ball, with the parchment paper still folded around it, into the Dutch oven and put the lid on.

7. Place the Dutch oven back into the stove and reduce the oven's temperature immediately to 400 degrees F.

8. Bake bread for 30 minutes, then remove the lid from the Dutch oven, as well as removing the parchment paper from the bread.

9. Bake the bread for a further 10 minutes and place bread on a wire cooling rack. Bread can be served warm or cold.

SIMPLE ROSEMARY BREAD

Prep Time: 2 ½ hours

Baking Time: 20 minutes

Total Time: 3 hours

Servings: 1 loaf

Equipment: Electric stand mixer with a dough hook, rimmed baking sheet

Ingredients:

- 1 ½ cups all-purpose flour
- ½ cup of warm water
- 2 tbsp olive oil
- 1 ⅛ tsp active dry yeast
- 1 ½ tsp sugar, white
- ½ tsp salt
- 1 ½ tbsp fresh rosemary, chopped
- Olive oil and ground black pepper for serving
- Sea salt (this is optional to sprinkle on top of the loaf)

Instructions:

1. Place the yeast, sugar, and warm water into the bowl of a stand mixer and stir to dissolve the yeast. Set aside until the yeast foams, about 5-10 minutes.

2. Add ¾ cup of flour, rosemary, 1 tbsp olive oil, and salt to the yeast mixture and combine well.

3. Fit the dough hook onto the mixer and add another ¾ cup of flour and mix until the dough is smooth and elastic on medium speed. Should the dough stick to the sides of the bowl, sprinkle extra flour in small amounts into the dough.

4. Cover the bowl with plastic wrap or a kitchen towel and set aside to rest in a warm part of the kitchen for about 1 ½ hour. Check to see if the dough has risen and doubled in size. It is ready when the dough has more than doubled.

5. Prepare a rimmed baking sheet by drizzling 1 tbsp olive oil on it and spreading the oil evenly across the baking sheet.

6. Shape the dough into an oval shape by pulling the edges of the dough towards the center. Tuck the edges in and place the bread onto the baking sheet, making sure the tucked in edges (the seam) is at the bottom and rests on the baking sheet.

7. Set the baking sheet with the bread aside to rise again for another hour, or until you see it has again doubled in size.

8. During the last part of the rising, preheat the oven to 400 degrees F.

9. Bake the bread in the center of the oven for 10 minutes. Remove from the oven and brush the remainder of the olive oil over the bread and sprinkle the bread with sea salt. Return the bread to the oven and bake until the loaf is golden brown, approximately 8-10 minutes.

10. Turn loaf out onto a wire cooling rack to cool down slightly before serving.

11. Serve warm with the black pepper and olive oil dip.

SWEET PEPPER AND CHEESE SPIRAL

Prep Time: 4 hours

Baking Time: 50 minutes

Total Time: 4 hours and 50 minutes

Servings: 1 loaf

Equipment: Electric stand mixer, Dutch oven or 9-inch round cake pan

Ingredients:

- ½ cup warm water (max 110 degrees F)
- 6 oz Monterey Jack cheese, shredded
- 6 oz Pepper Jack cheese, shredded
- 3 ¼ cup all-purpose flour
- ½ to 1 cup of sliced sweet piquante peppers (Peppadew)
- 2 eggs, large
- 1 egg yolk, large
- 1 egg, for egg wash, slightly beaten
- 4 tbsp melted, unsalted butter
- 1 ½ tsp red pepper flakes
- 1 ¼ tsp salt
- ¼ cup sugar, granulated
- 1 tbsp rapid rise yeast or instant yeast
- Red pepper flakes for topping

Instructions:

1. Add sugar, pepper flakes, flour, salt, and yeast to the bowl of a standing mixer and use the whisk attachment to combine.

2. Using a separate medium-sized bowl, add butter, water, eggs, and egg yolk and whisk.

3. Change the attachment of the electric mixer to the dough hook. Start the mixer on medium speed and slowly pour the wet mixture into the dry ingredients. Mix for about 10 minutes until the dough does not stick to the bottom and the sides of the mixing bowl anymore.

4. The dough should now be a smooth, soft ball. Place the dough ball into a prepared and greased bowl and cover the bowl with plastic wrap and set aside in a warm place in the kitchen to rise until dough has doubled. This takes about 1 ½ to 2 hours.

5. Place the dough onto a floured workspace. Make sure the workspace is sufficiently floured to prevent the dough from sticking. Roll the dough into a rectangle of about 12x18-inches. Spread the shredded cheese evenly across the dough and make sure to leave a 1-inch border clear. Place the sliced sweet piquante peppers on top of the cheese. Please note that the amount of sweet peppers used is totally according to personal preference, start with ½ cup and add more until you are satisfied with the amount used.

6. Roll the dough rectangle tightly into a log, starting from the long side to give a longer log.

7. Make sure the seam side of the log is at the bottom, then roll it into a spiral, taking care to tuck the end of the spiral under the loaf to prevent it from

coming loose during baking. Transfer the spiral to the bowl of a Dutch oven or a greased cake pan (9-inch), whichever of these two baking methods you are using.

8. Cover the bowl of dough with plastic wrap loosely or cover with a kitchen towel and set aside until it has risen to double its size, about 1 ½ to 2 hours.

9. Move the oven rack to the bottom position in the oven about 20 minutes before the end of the 2nd rising phase and preheat oven to 350 degrees F.

10. Brush the egg wash over the top of the dough and sprinkle red pepper flakes as a topping according to personal preference. Bake the bread for 25 minutes. Rotate the pan or Dutch oven and place an aluminum foil tent over the top of the cake pan or Dutch oven, making sure the tent fits loosely and is not tight fitting—Bake bread for an additional 25 minutes.

11. Cool the bread in the Dutch oven or cake pan until you can handle it without burning yourself and then transfer the bread to a wire cooling rack.

12. Serve warm or cold.

CHAPTER 5

KNEADED BREAD

Kneading is done either by hand or by using a stand mixer with a dough hook attachment. Each step in the kneading process must be followed to ensure well-risen and fluffy bread.

RUSTIC MUESLI BREAD

Prep Time: 3 hours

Baking Time: 25-35 minutes

Total Time: 3 hours and 35 minutes

Servings: 1 loaf

Equipment: Electric stand mixer (optional), flat metal or cast-iron pan

Ingredients:

- ¼ cup whole wheat flour
- 1 ½ cups warm water (max temperature 110 degrees F)
- 3 cups flour, unbleached
- ¾ tsp fast-acting yeast (do not substitute)
- ½ tsp salt
- ¼ cup raw or roasted almonds
- ¼ cup pumpkin seeds, raw
- ¼ cup raisins, brown or golden

Instructions:

1. Place the whole wheat and unbleached flour, salt, yeast and the warm water in a large mixing bowl and stir with a wooden spoon. If you are using a mixer, beat for 1 minute on medium speed. The dough will be rough and sticky; this is normal.

2. Prepare a bowl with olive oil or nonstick baking spray and place the dough in this bowl and cover with plastic wrap or a kitchen towel.

3. Rising time can be done in two ways. Place the covered bowl into the fridge for 2 hours to rise, or first, let it rise at room temperature for 2 hours and then place it in the fridge to let it rise for another 2 hours. Some bakers prefer the longer rising time, depending on their schedules and preference.

4. Lightly sprinkle the dough with flour, when rising time is done and tip out the dough onto a floured workspace. Knead the dough a few times to give it stretch and elasticity. Then add the raisins, pumpkin seeds, and almonds to the dough. Knead the dough again to incorporate the seeds and nuts. It is important to keep the seeds and nuts on the inside of the dough. If the seeds, and especially the raisins poke through the surface of the dough, these will become over-crisped and may burn. You will then have to remove them before serving the bread, as especially the raisins will have a bitter taste.

5. Grease and line a rimmed baking sheet with parchment paper and place the loaf on the paper. Sprinkle or sift a small amount of flour over the top of the bread. This is to help keep the dough from drying out. Set aside for 45-60 minutes to rest before baking.

6. Place a cast iron or metal pan into the oven on the lowest rack and preheat the oven up to 450 degrees F. Please do not use ceramic or glass containers.

7. Score the bread with a lame or a knife across the top. Make 2 or 3 cuts no deeper than ½-inch. You can also use kitchen shears to snip the top of the bread a few times.

8. Place the bread on the middle rack of the oven and pour the hot water carefully into the metal pan on the rack beneath the bread. The water will steam and bubble when it comes into contact with the hot metal pan, so close the oven door quickly to trap the steam inside.

9. Bake the bread for 25-35 minutes until the crust is golden brown or a deep brown, depending on how crisp you prefer the crust to be

10. Remove the bread from the baking sheet and place it on a wire cooling rack.

11. The bread can be stored at room temperature in an airtight container.

SUN DRIED TOMATO & OLIVE BREAD

Prep Time: 3 hours
Baking Time: 40 minutes
Total Time: 3 hours and 40 minutes
Servings: 1 loaf
Equipment: Stand electric mixer with a dough hook

Ingredients:

- 1 ½ - 1 ¾ cups bread flour
- 1 cup all-purpose flour, unbleached
- ½ cup yellow cornmeal
- 1 ½ tsp active dry yeast
- 1 ⅓ cups warm water (max 330-345 degrees F)
- ⅓ cup sun-dried tomatoes (in olive oil, drained and patted dry and chopped)
- 1 ½ tsp salt
- ⅓ cup kalamata olives (pitted, patted dry and quartered)
- 2 tbsp fresh basil, chopped
- ½ tsp sugar, granulated
- Olive oil, for brushing the top of the bread

Instructions:

1. Use a large mixing bowl or the bowl of the electric mixer. Add sugar, yeast, and 1 cup of warm water to the bowl and stir. Set aside until the yeast foams, about 10 minutes.

2. Add cornmeal, all-purpose flour, salt, and ¾ cup of bread flour to the yeast mixture and use a wooden spoon to combine until the mixture comes together.

3. To knead by hand, you turn the dough out on a well-floured workspace and knead the dough for about 10 minutes. During the kneading, add small amounts of the reserved bread flour until the dough is soft, only slightly sticky, elastic, and smooth. If using a stand mixer, attach the dough hook and knead on medium speed for 5 minutes, adding the reserved bread flour a little at a time.

4. Add the basil, sun-dried tomatoes, and olives to the dough by hand. Knead gently to get these ingredients spread evenly through the dough. Oil a large bowl and place the dough ball into the bowl, turning the dough a few times to make sure all the surfaces are coated in oil. Use plastic wrap to cover the bowl and set aside to allow the dough to rise for 1 to 1 ½ hour until the dough has doubled in size.

5. Line a rimmed baking sheet with parchment paper and give the baking sheet a light dusting of flour.

6. Punch down the bread dough and put the dough ball onto the baking sheet and pat the dough into an oval shape of approximately 10-by-8-inches. Do not handle the dough roughly. Bring the long side up and fold over towards the center and press the edge down into the center. Repeat this with the other long side of the dough and make sure to press the edge down into the center so that it sticks there.

7. Grease or spray plastic wrap with nonstick baking spray and cover the bread dough. Set aside in a warm part of the kitchen and leave the dough to rise for

45 minutes to 1 hour, until the dough has doubled in size.

8. Preheat the oven to 400 degrees F. Remove plastic cover from bread dough and use a pastry brush to lightly oil the bread. Bake in the center of the oven until the bread is a deep golden brown. To test if the bread is done, tap it on the bottom. If you hear a hollow sound, the bread is done.

9. Place bread on a wire cooling rack and slice once the bread has cooled down fully.

WALNUT & RAISIN PUMPERNICKEL

Prep Time: 1 hour and 10 minutes

Baking Time: 40 minutes

Total Time: 1 hour and 50 minutes

Servings: 1 large loaf

Equipment: Electric stand mixer with a dough hook, rimmed baking sheet, instant-read thermometer, and a pastry brush

Ingredients:

- 4 ½ cups bread flour
- 1 cup dark rye flour
- 1 ¾ cups warm water (max 110 degrees F)
- 2 ¼ tsp active dry yeast
- 2 tbsp instant coffee or espresso powder
- 1 cup almonds, toasted and chopped
- ¼ cup molasses
- 2 tsp salt
- 1 egg white
- 2 tbsp sugar, granulated
- 3 tbsp water
- ¾ cup raisins

Instructions:

1. Turn the oven on and heat to 200 degrees F.

2. Place yeast, water, and sugar into a large mixing bowl or the bowl of an electric mixer and stir with a wooden spoon until all the yeast has dissolved. Set aside for 5-10 minutes. The yeast is ready when it foams.

3. Add 4 cups of bread flour, instant coffee, rye flour, molasses, raisins, salt, and walnuts to the mixing bowl. Combine the mixture with a wooden spoon or use the dough hook of the electric mixer on low speed.

4. Flour a workspace and remove dough from the bowl. Knead the dough for 10 to 15 minutes here, adding the bread flour a little at a time until the dough is elastic and smooth. Please note that the dough will be slightly sticky. If using an electric mixer, knead the dough using the dough hook, on medium speed for about 5 minutes.

5. Line a rimmed baking sheet with parchment paper. Shape the bread into an oval shape of about 9 x 5-inches. Place the dough onto the baking sheet and cover with a clean kitchen towel. Leave the dough to rise for 30 minutes in the oven

6. Turn the oven off and place the baking sheet on the middle oven rack. Leave the bread in the oven for 30 minutes to rise and to double in size.

7. Remove the baking sheet from the oven and switch the oven back on and heat to 375 degrees F.

8. Make an egg wash with the egg yolk and water. Brush the egg wash over all the surfaces of the bread, and then score the top of the bread with a serrated knife three times to make slits of ¼ inch depth.

9. Bake the bread until it has a deep brown crust, about 35-40 minutes. Place an

instant-read thermometer into the middle of the bread. The bread is done when the thermometer reads 200 degrees F.

10. Place the bread on a wire cooling rack and serve warm or cold.

ONION BREAD

Prep Time: 1 ½ hour

Baking Time: 30 minutes

Total Time: 2 hours

Servings: 1 loaf

Equipment: 6 x 10-inch loaf pan, frying pan

Ingredients For Caramelized Onions:
- 1 bunch of chopped green onion bulbs
- 2 tbsp olive oil
- 1 large onion, thinly sliced or chopped
- Salt

Ingredients For Dough:
- 4 cups all-purpose flour
- 2 ¼ tsp active dry yeast
- 1 bunch of very finely chopped green onion leaves
- 1 ⅓ cup warm water
- 1 tsp salt
- Caramelized onion mixture

Instructions:
1. Place a frying pan on the cooktop and add olive oil and bring to medium heat. Add the onions to the pan and cook until the onions are soft and golden. Set the pan aside to allow the onion mixture to cool.

2. Place green onion leaves and the flour into a large mixing bowl.

3. Pour the warm water into a small mixing bowl and add the active dry yeast and let it stand for 5 to 10 minutes, until the yeast mixture foams.

4. Pour yeast mixture into the flour mixture and use a wooden spoon to mix.

5. Add the onion mixture and knead the dough in the bowl until the dough no longer clings to the sides of the bowl and the dough has a smooth texture.

6. Cover the bowl with plastic wrap or a kitchen towel and allow it to rise until the size of the dough has doubled. This will take about 1 hour.

7. Prepare a clean workspace by dusting it with flour. Transfer the dough to the workspace and roll the dough into a log shape. Place the dough into a greased and floured loaf pan and set aside for 30 minutes for the dough to rise.

8. Optional toppings to sprinkle over the dough are some of the onion leaves, finely chopped, and coarse salt.

9. Preheat the oven to 470 degrees F and place a small pot filled with water at the bottom of the oven. This is to create steam during the baking process.

10. Place the loaf pan in the center of the oven and bake for 15 minutes and then remove the pot of water.

11. Bring the oven temperature down to 450 degrees F and continue baking the bread for an extra 10-15 minutes.

12. Turn bread out onto a wire cooling rack. Allow the bread to cool down before slicing it.

OLIVE OIL AND RICOTTA BREAD WITH HERBS

Prep Time: 2 hours and 20 minutes

Baking Time: 40 minutes

Total Time: 3 hours

Servings: 1 loaf

Equipment: Electric stand mixer with a dough hook (optional), loaf pan

Ingredients:

- 2 tbsp all-purpose flour, unbleached
- 2 cups all-purpose flour, unbleached
- 1 ½ cups whole wheat flour
- ¼ cup water, lukewarm (max 110 degrees F)
- ¾ cup water, lukewarm
- ¼ cup olive oil
- 2 ¼ tsp active dry yeast (1 packet)
- ½ cup ricotta cheese
- 1 tsp oregano, dried
- 1 tsp salt
- 1 tsp basil, dried

Instructions:

1. Mix 2 tbsp flour, yeast, and ¼ cup lukewarm water together in a large mixing bowl or the bowl of a stand mixer. Set aside until mixture foams, about 5 minutes.

2. Add the following ingredients to the yeast mixture; ricotta cheese, herbs, olive oil, flours, and salt to the yeast mixture and stir to incorporate all the ingredients.

3. If using a mixer, attach the dough hook and start mixing at slow speed. Gradually add lukewarm water until the dough comes together and is no longer sticking to the sides of the mixing bowl. Increase mixer speed to medium and knead the dough until it becomes elastic and smooth about 3-5 minutes.

4. If mixing by hand, use a wooden spoon and stir lukewarm water into the mixing bowl slowly until the dough comes together and starts pulling away from the sides of the bowl. Transfer the dough to a prepared and floured workspace and knead the dough until it is elastic, and there are no lumps in the dough. This takes about 10-15 minutes.

5. Lightly oil a suitable bowl and place the dough ball into it. Cover the bowl with a kitchen towel or use plastic wrap that has been oiled slightly. Set the bowl aside in a warm part of the kitchen for the dough to rise and double in size. This takes roughly 1 hour.

6. Grease or spray a loaf pan with nonstick baking spray. Remove the dough from the rising bowl and press the dough into a square of 9x9 inches. Roll the dough square tightly into a log and tuck the edges underneath, making sure the top of the dough is smooth. Place the dough log into the oiled loaf pan and lightly cover with a kitchen towel or plastic wrap that has been oiled. Set the loaf pan aside and allow the dough to rise and double in size for the second time for about 1 hour.

7. Set the oven to 375 degrees F to preheat. Remove the covering from the dough and place loaf pan in the center of the oven and bake for 30-40 minutes. Check with an instant-read thermometer by inserting it into the bread. The bread is done when the thermometer registers 200 degrees F.

8. Remove the loaf pan from the oven and allow the bread to cool in the pan for 10 minutes, then remove the bread and set it to cool down completely on a wire cooling rack. Slice and serve bread once it has cooled down completely.

CHAPTER 6

CRUSTY ROLLS

Artisan rolls come in all shapes and sizes and variety, from plain crusty rolls, savory rolls, and soft pull-apart rolls. Artisan rolls are not difficult to make and are welcomed at any meal.

CRUSTY WHITE ROLLS

Prep Time: 3 hours and 35 minutes

Baking Time: 25 minutes

Total Time: 4 hours

Servings: 8 rolls

Equipment: Baking pan, rubber or silicone spatula

Ingredients:

- 2 ½ cups all-purpose or bread flour
- 1 ¼ cups warm water (max 130 degrees F)
- 1 tsp salt
- ¼ tsp active dry yeast or instant yeast

Instructions:

1. Place all the dry ingredients into a large mixing bowl. Gradually pour in the water and stir mixture with a wooden spoon. Please note that this is a sticky and quite thick dough.

2. Cover with a kitchen towel or plastic wrap and set aside for 3 hours to rise. The dough will have bubbles on the top when it is ready.

3. Prepare a workspace and lightly dust it with flour. Turn the dough out onto the floured surface. Fold the dough over on itself 12 times with a rubber spatula. Dust the dough to prevent the dough from sticking.

4. Cut the dough ball into 8 pieces with a rubber scraper or spatula. Dust your hands with flour and shape each of the pieces of dough into balls by folding and then tucking the edges underneath.

5. Place the 8 rolls into a baking pan lined with parchment paper. Cover the rolls with a kitchen towel and set aside for 35 minutes at room temperature. Please note the rolls will not double in size but will be puffy.

6. While the rolls are resting, preheat the oven to 450 degrees F. Make sure the oven temperature is accurate at 450 degrees F before baking the rolls.

7. Place the baking pan in the center of the oven and bake the rolls until they are golden brown and crisp. This takes about 25-30 minutes.

8. Remove the rolls from the oven onto a wire cooling rack before serving.

9. The rolls can easily be re-crisped again if they have not been eating on the day of baking. Heat the oven to 325 degrees F and place the rolls in the oven (do not use a baking pan, place rolls directly onto the oven rack) and leave rolls in the oven for 10-12 minutes and then serve.

HOAGIE ROLLS

Prep Time: 1 hour and 40 minutes

Baking Time: 20 minutes

Total Time: 2 hours

Servings: 8 rolls

Equipment: Electric stand mixer (optional), pastry brush, silicone baking mat (optional)

Ingredients:

- 4 to 4 ½ cups all-purpose flour (divided)
- 3 tsp granulated sugar (divided)
- 2 tbsp vegetable oil
- 3 tbsp water
- 1 ½ cups warm water (max 115 degrees F) (divided)
- 1 ½ tsp salt
- 1 tsp salt
- 2 ¼ tsp active dry yeast (1 packet)
- 2 tbsp butter, unsalted, melted and cooled down
- 1 ½ cups Asiago cheese, shredded (see Notes)
- 1 egg yolk
- ½ tsp garlic powder
- 1 clove of garlic, minced finely
- 2 tsp Italian seasoning
- ½ tsp onion powder

Instructions:

1. Place the yeast and 2 tsp sugar into a large mixing bowl or the bowl of a stand mixer. Add ½ cup warm water to the yeast and stir with a wooden spoon until the yeast has dissolved. Set aside for 5 minutes until the yeast mixture becomes foamy.

2. Add the remaining water, 3 cups of flour, salt, oil, and residual sugar to the yeast mixture and stir with a wooden spoon until the ingredients are combined.

3. Attach the dough hook to the mixer and knead the dough on medium power for about 5 minutes and add small amounts of the remaining flour during the kneading until the dough is elastic and smooth with no lumps. Please note that this dough is slightly sticky, so do not add too much flour.

4. If kneading by hand, place the dough on a well-floured working surface and knead for 10 minutes by hand. Add small amounts of flour during the kneading process until the dough is smooth, no longer very sticky, and elastic.

5. Form the dough into a ball and place it into a lightly oiled bowl, making sure to turn the bowl to ensure the surface is completely coated and cover the bowl with plastic wrap or a kitchen towel. Set the bowl aside in a warm place in the kitchen for 1 hour until the dough has doubled in size.

6. Tip the dough ball out onto a floured workspace and punch the dough down. Divide the dough into 8 pieces and form 8 oval-shaped rolls, roughly 5 inches in length. Place the rolls on a greased baking pan or use a silicone baking mat in the baking pan. Make sure that the rolls are well separated from each other with about 2 inches of space between the rolls.

7. Make slashes across the tops of the rolls with a serrated knife or lame, or snip into the rolls with kitchen shears. Incisions should be roughly ¼-inch in depth. Cover the rolls with a kitchen towel or oiled plastic wrap and set aside until the dough has nearly doubled in size and has puffed up. This takes about 30 minutes

8. Preheat the oven to 400 degrees F while the rolls are rising.

9. Whisk the melted butter, garlic powder, minced garlic, salt, water, onion powder, Italian seasoning, and egg yolk together in a medium-sized mixing bowl. When the rolls are ready for the oven, use a pastry brush to cover the rolls with this mixture, coating every side and the tops. Lastly, sprinkle the rolls with Asiago cheese.

10. Place the baking pan in the center of the oven and bake rolls for 20 minutes and rotate the pan once or twice during the baking process. The rolls are done when the tops are browned, and the cheese has melted.

11. Place rolls on a wire cooling rack to cool down. The rolls will slice easier if you allow them to cool down completely first.

Notes:

Asiago cheese might be difficult to find locally in the area where you live. The following cheeses are great substitutes for any recipe that requires Asiago cheese:

1. Monterey Jack cheese
2. Dry Jack cheese
3. Parmesan
4. Grana Padano
5. Gruyere
6. Romano
7. Provolone

CHEDDAR BRIOCHE BUNS WITH GARLIC

Prep Time: 2 hours and 40 minutes

Baking Time: 25 - 30 minutes

Total Time: 3 hours and 10 minutes

Servings: 12 buns

Equipment: Stand mixer with a dough hook (optional)

Ingredients:

- 2 ¾ cups bread or all-purpose flour (plus extra)
- 1 ½ tbsp instant yeast
- 1 egg yolk
- 3 eggs
- 1 egg for egg wash
- 1 tbsp water for egg wash
- ¼ cup dry milk powder (full fat or nonfat as per personal preference)
- ¼ cup of warm water (max 115 degrees F) (plus extra)
- 3 tbsp sugar, granulated
- 10 tbsp butter, unsalted and softened (grate or chop into tiny cubes)
- 2 tsp minced garlic
- 1 cup cheddar cheese, shredded
- 1 ½ tsp salt
- Coarse salt for sprinkling over buns

Instructions:

1. Place sugar, dry milk powder, yeast, and flour into a large mixing bowl or the bowl of a stand mixer and whisk to combine. Add cheddar cheese, garlic, butter, egg yolk, eggs, warm water, and salt. Use the dough hook and low speed to combine the ingredients or stir with a wooden spoon.

2. Set mixer speed to medium for 5 minutes and knead the dough. Add small amounts of water or flour as needed, work sparingly. The dough is ready when it starts to pull away and no longer cling to the sides of the bowl. This is a slightly sticky dough, so do not use too much flour, you do not want a dry dough. The dough is ready when it has a smooth texture and is elastic.

3. If kneading by hand, put the dough on a floured work surface and proceed to knead until the dough is elastic with a smooth texture and still slightly sticky. This takes about 10 minutes.

4. Form a ball and place the dough ball into a bowl that has been oiled or sprayed with nonstick baking spray. Turn the dough around to make sure all surfaces have an oily coating. Cover the bowl with a kitchen towel or oiled plastic wrap. Set aside to enable the dough to double in size, about 1 ½ to 2 hours.

5. Line a baking pan with parchment paper, dust with flour and set aside. Punch down the dough and divide it into 12 equal-sized balls. Shape each ball to have a rounded top and cover with plastic wrap or a kitchen towel. Set the baking pan aside for the dough to rise to nearly doubled in size, roughly 30-40 minutes.

6. Preheat the oven to 375 degrees F.

7. Score the buns with a lame, or kitchen shears, or serrated knife and make two cuts on top of each bun. Use a pastry brush to cover the buns with the prepared egg wash of whisked egg and water. Lastly, sprinkle salt over the buns. This is optional as per personal preference.

8. Bake until the buns are a deep golden brown and puffed up, for about 25-30 minutes.

9. Turn buns out onto a wire cooling rack. Buns can be eaten warm or cold.

PUMPKIN PULL-APART ROLLS

Prep Time: 3 hours and 15 minutes

Baking Time: 25 minutes

Total Time: 3 hours and 45 minutes

Servings: 12 rolls

Equipment: Stand mixer with a dough hook, 9-inch round or square baking pan

Ingredients:

- 2 ½ cups all-purpose flour (plus extra)
- ⅜ cup milk brought to room temperature
- 1 egg, small
- 1 tsp instant yeast
- half of a 15 oz. can pumpkin purée
- 1 ½ tsp salt, kosher or sea salt
- 2 tbsp sugar
- nutmeg, fresh and grated to personal preference
- pinch of cloves, ground
- ½ tsp cinnamon
- ¼ tsp ginger, ground
- butter to grease pan

Instructions:

1. Add yeast, 1 tsp of the sugar, and the milk to a large mixing bowl or the bowl of a stand mixer. Set aside for 15 minutes for the yeast to develop.

2. Place all the remaining ingredients for this recipe in the mixing bowl, except the egg and the butter. Attach the dough hook and start the mixer on low speed and mix the dough for 10 minutes. Add flour to the dough slowly until the dough no longer sticks to the sides of the mixing bowl. The dough is ready when it does not stick to the sides or the bottom of the bowl.

3. Remove the dough from the mixing bowl and place it in an oiled or greased bowl. Cover the bowl with plastic wrap or a kitchen towel and set aside for the dough to rise. The dough is ready when it has doubled in size, about 2 hours.

4. Prepare a floured work surface. Punch down the risen dough and place the dough on the surface—grease a 9x9-inch baking pan with the butter. Make 10-12 even sized dough balls into the baking pan and make sure you space them apart to allow for rising. Cover the baking pan with a kitchen towel or plastic wrap and set aside for the dough to rise for 1 hour or until the dough balls have doubled in size.

5. Preheat the oven to 400 degrees F. Place the baking pan in the center of the oven and bake pumpkin rolls for 20 minutes.

6. While the rolls are baking, prepare the egg wash with the egg and ½ tsp water.

7. Remove the baking pan after 20 minutes and use a pastry brush to coat the rolls with the egg mixture. Return the baking pan to the oven and bake for 5 minutes.

8. Remove pumpkin rolls from the baking pan and set on a wire cooling rack, or a serving board or plate.

9. Serve immediately with softened butter.

MUFFIN PAN THYME ROLLS

Prep Time: 2 hours and 20 minutes

Baking Time: 30 minutes

Total Time: 2 hours and 50 minutes

Servings: 12 rolls

Equipment: 12-cup muffin pan

Ingredients:

- 4 cups unbleached all-purpose flour
- 2 tsp sugar
- 1-2 tbsp fresh thyme, minced
- 2 tsp salt, sea salt or kosher
- 2 tsp instant yeast
- 2 tbsp butter, at room temperature
- 2 cups water, lukewarm (max 110 degrees F)

Instructions:

1. Please note that this is a very messy dough, so be prepared for it.

2. Mix the salt, instant yeast, flour, sugar, and fresh thyme in a large mixing bowl. A whisk is best to use and make sure that all the flour has been fully incorporated. Cover with a kitchen towel or plastic wrap and set aside to rise for 1 ½ to 2 hours.

3. Oil or butter a 12-cup muffin pan, plus a few ramekins as you may have extra dough leftover.

4. Preheat the oven to 425 degrees F.

5. Punch down the dough using two forks, scraping the dough from the sides of the bowl. Make sure the dough is punched down well, so use the two forks to fold the dough over onto itself as you rotate the mixing bowl and scraping the sides.

6. Turn the dough out onto a floured work surface and divide the dough into 6 portions with the forks. Divide each portion again into two forks and scoop into the muffin cups. Any leftover dough can be scooped into the ramekins. Allow the dough to rise in the muffin pan for 17-20 minutes. Check up on the rising dough; it is ready when the dough shows slightly above the rim of the muffin cups.

7. Bake at 435 degrees F for 15 minutes and then turn the heat down to 375 degrees F. Continue baking the rolls for an extra 10-15 minutes. Turn the rolls out onto a wire cooling rack to cool down for a few minutes.

8. Serve warm with butter.

CHAPTER 7

OVEN BAKED BREADS

Certain artisan styles of bread are best suited to bake in the oven, such as loaves and oval bread. Oven baking does not necessarily take longer than a Dutch oven, and you have an endless variety to experiment with.

BACON AND CHEESE BREAD

Prep Time: 1 hour and 40 minutes

Baking Time: 60 minutes

Total Time: 2 hours and 40 minutes

Servings: 1 loaf

Equipment: Loaf pan

Ingredients:

- 3 cups all-purpose flour
- 1 tsp instant yeast
- 1 tsp sugar
- 1 ½ cups warm water
- 1 tsp salt
- 1 cup cheddar cheese, preferably freshly grated (reserve some for topping)
- 5 strips of thick-cut bacon, cooked and chopped (reserve some for topping)
- ground pepper to taste

Instructions:

1. Add yeast, sugar, water, and salt to a large mixing bowl. Set aside for 5 minutes.

2. Remember to reserve some bacon and cheese to sprinkle over the bread.

3. Add bacon, flour, cheese, and pepper to the yeast mixture and stir with a wooden spoon to combine ingredients. This is a rough dough at this stage but comes together at a later stage.

4. Cover the bowl with a kitchen towel or plastic wrap and set aside in a warm part of the kitchen for 1 hour.

5. Prepare a floured working space and tip dough out. Knead the dough only long enough so that it holds together. Place the dough into an oiled loaf pan and sprinkle the reserved bacon and cheese over the top of the dough. Cover the loaf pan and allow the dough to rise for 30 minutes.

6. Heat oven to 400 degrees F and bake the bread for 15 minutes. Reduce the heat to 350 degrees F and place a sheet of foil loosely over the top of the loaf pan and continue baking the bread for 35 minutes. Remove the foil sheet and continue baking for an extra 10 minutes.

OLIVE LOAF

Prep Time: 2 hours and 30 minutes

Baking Time: 30 minutes

Total Time: 3 hours

Servings: 1 loaf

Equipment: Stand mixer with a dough hook, 2 baking sheets

Ingredients:

- 2 ¾ cup flour, all-purpose
- 2 tsp olive oil
- 1 ½ tsp instant yeast
- ½ tsp garlic powder
- 1 cup water, lukewarm
- ½ cup Kalamata olives, pitted and chopped

Instructions:

1. Place all the ingredients, except the olives, into the bowl of an electric mixer and stir with a wooden spoon to combine. Set aside for 15 minutes to allow the yeast to bloom.

2. Attach the dough hook to the stand mixer and add the olives to the bowl. Knead for 5 minutes on medium speed. If the dough clings to the sides of the bowl, sprinkle small amounts of flour on the dough until it releases.

3. Oil a mixing bowl and place the dough into this bowl and cover with plastic wrap or a kitchen towel. Set aside in a warm part of the kitchen to rise for 60 minutes.

4. Line a baking sheet with parchment paper.

5. Place dough on a floured work surface and punch dough down and place on the prepared baking sheet. Shape the dough into an oval shape and cover the dough with a kitchen cloth. Set aside for 60 minutes to rise again.

6. Heat the oven to 400 degrees F and place a second rimmed baking sheet on the bottom oven rack.

7. Give the dough a slight dusting of flour and score three times with a lame or a serrated knife across the top.

8. Place the baking sheet with the bread dough on the center rack in the oven and pour ½ of water into the baking sheet on the bottom rack and close the oven door quickly—Bake bread for 30 minutes.

9. Place bread on a wire cooling rack and allow it to cool down completely before slicing.

BREAD WITH SUNFLOWER SEEDS

Prep Time: 3 hours

Baking Time: 40 minutes

Total Time: 3 hours and 40 minutes

Servings: 1 loaf

Equipment: Loaf pan 8 x 4-inch, stand mixer with a dough hook

Ingredients:

- 1 cup all-purpose flour, unbleached
- 1 cup whole wheat flour
- ⅔ cup warm water or milk
- ½ tsp active dry yeast
- 1 tbsp honey
- 1 tbsp plus 1 tsp vegetable oil (canola or olive)
- 2 tsp sugar
- 1 egg
- ½ tsp salt
- ⅓ cup sunflower seeds, plus extra to use as a topping

Instructions:

1. Place yeast, milk, egg, salt, oil, honey, and sugar into the bowl of the mixer and stir with a wooden spoon to combine.

2. Add the sunflower seeds and flour and mix on low or medium speed until the dough no longer clings to the sides.

3. Transfer the dough to a greased or oiled mixing bowl and cover. Set aside 2 hours to rise. The dough should double in size.

4. Shape the loaf into a log or oval shape and transfer to the greased loaf pan. Set aside again to rise for 30-40 minutes. The dough should double in size.

5. Preheat the oven to 375 degrees F.

6. Use a pastry brush and coat the top of the loaf with vegetable oil and sprinkle the sunflower seeds on top.

7. Place the loaf on the center rack in the oven and bake for 35-40 minutes.

8. Turn bread out onto a wire cooling rack. Leave the bread to cool down fully before slicing.

BLUEBERRY BREAD

Prep Time: 2 hours and 30 minutes

Baking Time: 25 minutes

Total Time: 2 hours and 55 minutes

Servings: 1 loaf

Equipment: 8 x 5-inch loaf pan

Ingredients:

- 1 ½ cups bread flour
- 1 ⅛ tsp active dry yeast
- ⅜ cup milk (type per personal preference)
- 1 ½ tbsp water
- 1 tbsp butter, cut into cubes of 1-inch, brought to room temperature
- 1 egg, small
- 1 ½ tbsp sugar
- 1 ½ tbsp dried blueberries (or more per personal preference)
- ⅜ tsp salt
- ⅛ tsp nutmeg

Instructions:

1. Mix yeast, flour, salt, sugar, and nutmeg in a large mixing bowl.

2. In a separate bowl, mix butter, milk, water, and egg.

3. Add wet ingredients to the bowl holding the dry ingredients and mix.

4. Add blueberries to the dough mixture and stir with a wooden spoon until a rough dough forms. Turn the dough out onto a flour work surface and knead for 10 minutes until the dough is smooth and soft.

5. Place dough in an oiled mixing bowl and cover. Set aside to rise for about 60-90 minutes, until the dough has doubled in size.

6. Punch the dough down and then form into a loaf and place it into an oiled or greased loaf pan 8 x 5-inch and cover. Set aside to rise for 1 hour until the dough has doubled in size.

7. Heat oven to 350 degrees F and place loaf pan on the center rack of the oven. Bake for 20-25 minutes, until golden brown.

8. Place bread pan on a wire cooling rack. Do not remove bread from the pan until it has cooled down completely. Slice and serve.

CONCLUSION

You now have all the necessary information about the basics of baking artisan bread and all the do's and don'ts to start making great tasting bread at home. The recipes are easy and versatile to allow for both oven baking and Dutch oven baking to please everyone.

The most important thing to take from this is that there is no reason at all why a beginner baker cannot make delicious tasting bread from scratch. Remember, even the master bakers had to spend time learning and made plenty of mistakes along the way. If the occasional hiccup comes along, work around it, make a few changes and keep baking!

Made in the USA
Middletown, DE
08 October 2020